The Story of
TRAILBLAZING
IRA ALDRIDGE

by **Glenda Armand**

with illustrations by
Floyd Cooper

Lee & Low Books Inc.
New York

To my sister, Jenny, who quoted Shakespeare
as we did our chores—G.A.

To those who use their art to make a difference—F.C.

Acknowledgment

Special thanks to Bernth Lindfors, Professor Emeritus of English and African Literatures, University of Texas at Austin for reviewing the manuscript.

Author's Note

This story is true to the known facts of Ira Aldridge's life and the realities of society during the time he lived. However, in crafting this biography, I included some imagined scenes, people, thoughts, and dialogue. These parts of the story are dramatic extensions of historically documented events and interactions.

Text from *Ira's Shakespeare Dream* copyright © 2015 by Glenda Armand
Sidebar text by Glenda Armand copyright © 2019 by Lee & Low Books Inc.
Illustrations copyright © 2015 by Floyd Cooper
Photo credits: p. 10: public domain • p. 19: Schomburg Center for Research in Black Culture, Photographs and Prints Division, The New York Public Library. "The African Grove Theatre in Greenwich Village, ca. 1821." New York Public Library Digital Collections. • p. 26: public domain • p. 35: Georgios Kollidas / Shutterstock.com • p. 39: public domain • p. 45: Beinecke Rare Book & Manuscript Library, Yale University Library. "Ira Aldridge as Othello." Beineke Digital Collections.

LEE & LOW BOOKS Inc., 95 Madison Avenue, New York, NY 10016
leeandlow.com
Edited by Jessica V. Echeverria and Kandace Coston
Book design by Abhi Alwar
Book production by The Kids at Our House
Manufactured in the United States of America by Lake Book Manufacturing, Inc.
The text is set in Vollkorn.
The display font is set in Avenir.
The illustrations are rendered in oil wash with kneaded erasures.
10 9 8 7 6 5 4 3 2 1
First Edition

Library of Congress Cataloging-in-Publication Data

Names: Armand, Glenda, author. | Cooper, Floyd, illustrator.
Title: The story of trailblazing actor Ira Aldridge / by Glenda Armand with illustrations by Floyd Cooper.
Description: First edition. | New York : Lee & Low Books, [2019] | Includes bibliographical references.
Identifiers: LCCN 2019020607 | ISBN 9781643790084 (paperback)
Subjects: LCSH: Aldridge, Ira Frederick, -1867--Juvenile literature. | Shakespearean actors and actresses--Biography--Juvenile literature. | African American actors--Biography--Juvenile literature.
Classification: LCC PN2598.A52 A76 2019 | DDC 792.02/8092 [B] --dc23
LC record available at https://lccn.loc.gov/2019020607

TABLE OF CONTENTS

CHAPTER ONE
YOUNG PERFORMER

Ira could not keep still while he waited in the balcony of the Park Theatre. But once the magnificent velvet curtains opened, Ira sat **spellbound** as Shakespeare's play *Hamlet* was brought to life. Ira mouthed the words along with the actors:

This above all,— to thine own self be true...

After the final curtain came down, Ira hurried out of the theater. If he got home too late, Pa would know where he had been. Besides, Ira had

> **UNDERSTANDING SHAKESPEARE**
> ### *Hamlet*
>
> As an old man named Polonius prepares for his son's return to boarding school, he offers the young man some words of wisdom: Be a good listener, but don't talk too much. Never borrow or lend money, for that can end friendships. Dress well, but not in a flashy way. Finally, Polonius **summarizes** all of his advice in just a few words:
>
> **This above all,—to thine own self be true**
>
> *The Tragedy of Hamlet, Prince of Denmark*, Act I, Scene 3:78

to prepare for his own performance in class. "Tomorrow is my big day," he said to himself.

Ira Frederick Aldridge was born in 1807 in New York City at a time when most African Americans were still enslaved throughout the United States. He attended the African Free School, which was **founded** in 1787 to educate children of slaves and free people of color.

The next morning Ira **barreled** his way through the crowded New York City streets to the African Free School. When he arrived, he stood outside the classroom to catch his breath. Then he made his grand entrance.

"Ah, here he is," Ira's teacher, Mr. Andrews, announced to two men who were standing at the back of the room. "Students and honored guests, Ira Aldridge will now perform a scene from *Hamlet*, a play, as you all know, by the great William Shakespeare."

Ira paced back and forth, rubbing his chin and motioning with his arms as he spoke the words of Hamlet, the troubled young Danish prince.

To be, or not to be: that is the question—

UNDERSTANDING SHAKESPEARE

Hamlet

Prince Hamlet is angry, sad, and confused. His father has been murdered and Hamlet believes that it was King Claudius who killed him. And now, King Claudius is married to Hamlet's mother! In **contemplating** this dreadful situation, the prince cannot decide whether it would be better to live or to die:

To be, or not to be: that is the question—
The Tragedy of Hamlet, Prince of Denmark, Act III, Scene 1:56

"Bravo!" cheered his classmates and the visitors after Ira ended the scene with a bow.

"Such talent!" said one of the visitors.

"For one so young, you have a great voice," added the other. "And your gestures perfectly matched the words!"

After school, Ira was still beaming as he helped Mr. Andrews clean the classroom. Suddenly Ira stopped sweeping. "I want to perform Shakespeare at the Park Theatre!" he exclaimed.

"The Park?" Mr. Andrews raised his eyebrows. "Ira, you know only white actors perform there. You dream too big for a colored boy."

"But the visitors said I have talent. My color did not matter to them!"

"They are from England, where things are different," explained Mr. Andrews. "Why not become a teacher here? You can use your great talent to inspire the younger students."

"I will inspire them by becoming a Shakespearean actor," Ira declared.

"And today I will tell Pa about my dream."

The African Free School

The years after the **American Revolution** were **momentous** for African Americans living in New York. In 1785, a group of wealthy New Yorkers who were committed to improving the circumstances and opportunities for black New Yorkers founded *The New York Society for the* **Manumission** *of Slaves and the Protection of such of Them as had been or wanted to be* **Liberated.** In 1799, the state government began passing a series of laws that would steadily free all enslaved people living in the state by July 4, 1827. The New York Manumission Society supported this legislation.

One of the first tasks of the Manumission Society was to protest and prevent the practice of kidnapping African Americans (enslaved and free) to take them down south and sell them into slavery. The Manumission Society also provided free legal help to black New Yorkers. But the Society's most lasting accomplishment was the establishment of the school that Ira Aldridge attended: the African Free School.

Black parents welcomed the African Free School. They were dissatisfied with the education their children were receiving in **segregated** and inferior public schools. These "colored schools," as they were called, offered basic literacy and focused on preparing African American children for low-skilled labor.

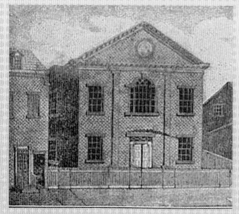

An engraving of the New York African Free School, by Patrick Henry Reason, 1830.

The African Free School had a higher mission, which was to form men and women "of **distinction**." The school empowered its students by **instilling** them with the confidence they needed to seek greater opportunities, and it offered a **rigorous curriculum** to prepare them. In addition to reading, writing, penmanship, arithmetic, literature, and scripture, students studied the physical sciences, natural history, astronomy, navigation, and geography. Students also learned practical trades such as knitting, sewing, sailmaking and carpentry. As a private institution, the African Free School charged between twenty-five cents to one dollar per quarter school year, depending upon the circumstances of the parents. The children of those who could not afford to pay were admitted free of charge and received the same instruction as paying students. Parents believed that with an education from the African Free School, their children could claim all the rights and benefits of full citizenship. They hoped that their children would not experience the kind of **prejudice** that they endured on a regular basis.

Ira Aldridge attended the Mulberry Street campus of the African Free School from 1820 to 1824. During that time, the school became a source of pride for the black community. Students frequently recited poems and essays and took oral examinations before the school's delighted **benefactors**. In 1824, a group of African Free School students and teachers traveled to Baltimore, Maryland to participate in the American Convention for Promoting the **Abolition** of Slavery and Improving the Condition of the African Race. At the convention, the students presented their original work, including poems written about slavery and freedom.

As the school's reputation grew, the African Free School became a frequent stop of visiting **dignitaries**. One such visitor was the Marquis de Lafayette of

France, who had fought alongside George Washington in the American Revolution. The students welcomed Lafayette with speeches, **recitals**, and displays of their scholarship.

In 1835, the African Free School became a part of the New York City public school system. By that time, it had grown from a one-room schoolhouse to seven buildings, and it had educated more than a thousand boys and girls. Besides Ira Aldridge, the school had many distinguished **alumni**, including African American **engraver** Patrick Henry Reason, who made a sketch of the African Free School for the cover of a book about the school when he was 13 years old.

Another distinguished graduate was James McCune Smith, the first African American physician. Dr. Smith looked back fondly at his time at the African Free School. Speaking of one of his teachers at the school, Smith said "He taught his boys and girls to look upward; to believe themselves capable of accomplishing as much as any others could, and to regard the higher walks of life as within their reach."

CHAPTER TWO

WAITING IN THE WINGS

Ira's father was a church **minister** who also sold items made of straw. Ira found Pa on Mulberry Street and sat with him in his wagon.

"Shakespeare!" Pa exclaimed, when Ira told him of his dream. "How can you make a living playacting and pretending? Your brother, Joshua, couldn't do it. What makes you think you can?"

Before Ira could answer, Pa began calling out to **passersby** in his **melodic** voice, "Straw man! Straw man! Get your baskets, hats, and mats!"

Ira sat patiently while Pa sold his wares. On the way home Pa said, "Ira, I want you to follow in my footsteps and become a minister. Use your God-given talent to preach about right and wrong. And stay away from that playhouse. What would your mother say about such foolishness?"

If Mama was alive, thought Ira, *she wouldn't call my dream foolish.*

Against Pa's wishes, Ira continued to go to the theater. He even discovered a new playhouse, the African Grove. It was the first all-black theater in New York City.

At the Park, Ira was forced to watch plays from the balcony. But at the Grove he could sit in any seat in the theater to watch the lively acts and musical numbers. Sometimes the Grove even staged all-black versions of Shakespeare's plays.

Ira was fascinated by the wigs, makeup, and colorful costumes worn by the actors. He longed to be a part of this magical world of the theater. *Why couldn't Pa understand?* Ira thought.

One day, feeling hopeless, Ira went to the waterfront to visit Joshua. Ira found him at work **whitewashing** a boat. As the brothers talked, Ira watched ships depart for far-off places such as England, the land of Shakespeare.

"You have more talent than I had," Joshua said, following his brother's gaze. "If any one of our people could become a successful actor, it would be you."

Just then the captain of a nearby cargo ship walked up. He told the brothers that he was leaving for South Carolina and needed a cabin boy to do chores on the trip. Ira looked at Joshua.

"Go. You need an adventure," Joshua said. "But be careful. Things are different down South."

"I will," Ira promised. "Tell Pa I'll be back soon!"

The African Grove Theatre

In the early nineteenth century, white New Yorkers frequented public spots called pleasure gardens. On a summer's day, visitors could find shade, recreation, and entertainment. These gardens were not open to African Americans.

In 1816, William Brown, a black **playwright**, actor, and former ship's **steward**, decided to create a public space for African Americans. He knew that when ships docked in New York, African American stewards would be in search of recreation. Brown bought a house located on Thomas Street in New York City. He transformed the house's yard into a pleasure garden that catered to African American stewards.

In addition to stewards, the pleasure garden attracted other African Americans in the community. In fact, Brown welcomed people of any race who were looking to spend a Sunday afternoon eating ice cream and drinking punch while listening to poetry, music, and dramatic pieces.

The dramatic presentations in the garden became so popular that in 1821 Brown bought a bigger, two-story house on Mercer Street, about a mile away. He converted the house into a theater that could seat three hundred people and named it the African Grove. It became the first theater built by a black man to serve African Americans. It was here that young Ira Aldridge began his acting career, working alongside the most famous black actor of the day, James Hewlett.

The African Grove was located near the Park Theatre. With its beautiful interior and two thousand seats, the Park was the **premier** theater in the City, offering high-quality Shakespearean performances. African Americans were allowed to attend performances at the Park but they were forced to sit in the balcony. With the arrival of the African Grove, black theatergoers now had a choice of **venues** when seeking entertainment.

To make his business profitable, William Brown had to charge Grove visitors more than the twenty-five cent price of admission to the Park. Brown hoped that African Americans would be willing to pay between thirty-seven to fifty cents for admission to the Grove, where they would be treated with respect. In the case of ship stewards who earned ten dollars a week, fifty cents might not be a hardship. But for a maid, fifty cents could be half a week's salary. Still, Brown guessed correctly—African Americans willingly paid his prices.

Some white people chose to attend performances at the African Grove, but it was often to mock the entertainment. Even at the Grove, white and black patrons were separated—whites sat behind a partition in the back of the theater.

Playbill from the African Grove Theatre in Greenwich Village, circa 1821.

The owner of the Park, Stephen Price, was unhappy when the African Grove began taking away some of his business. He hired people to interrupt performances at the Grove. These troublemakers destroyed property, **harassed** audience members, and physically attacked the actors. This created a **ruckus**. Policemen were called and the theater often had to shut down for the night. These disturbances happened so frequently that William Brown lost business. In 1826, a fire destroyed the African Grove and the theater was closed for good.

CHAPTER THREE
STAGESTRUCK

Ira enjoyed the voyage. But when the ship reached the port of Charleston, South Carolina, Ira was reminded of Joshua's warning. A man came aboard and, seeing Ira at work, offered to buy him for five hundred dollars.

At first Ira was angry at the idea of being sold like a basket or a straw hat. Then he became fearful. *Would the captain turn down so much money?* Ira wondered. He was relieved to hear the captain tell the slave trader, "This young man is not for sale."

Although Ira had been spared, he watched helplessly as other people were sold into slavery. He would never forget seeing men, women, and children on the auction block. He felt the **agony** of family members when they were sold off one by one and taken away by different owners.

Ira was happy to return to New York three weeks later. Facing Pa's anger would be easy after what he had seen down South.

After **scolding** Ira for running away, Pa said, "You will go to ministry school as soon as you are old enough!"

But Ira was determined to follow his dream. At the African Grove and the Park, people took notice of the **stagestruck** young man. Actors often sent Ira on errands in exchange for tickets to plays. Some of the stagehands taught him set building and costume making. They all encouraged Ira to become an actor and cheered him on as he **auditioned** for a small role at the African Grove.

When he was not watching plays from the balcony of the Park, Ira was rehearsing or acting

at the African Grove. He was soon chosen to play
the lead in Shakespeare's *Romeo and Juliet.*

It wasn't long before Pa discovered that Ira
had stopped going to school. He immediately
enrolled Ira in a ministry college. Now Ira was
faced with a difficult question: should he obey his
father or follow his own path?

The answer came from two actors who had
befriended Ira, the brothers James and Henry
Wallack. They were preparing to return to their

native country, England.

"You might find success as a Shakespearean actor in London," Henry Wallack said. "And we could use some help on the voyage. Would you like to come along as our **valet**?"

"Yes, sir!" Ira exclaimed. "I have experience working on a ship."

A line from *Romeo and Juliet* came to mind as Ira tearfully said good-bye to Joshua: *Parting is such sweet sorrow.*

In 1824, at the age of seventeen, Ira set sail for England. He looked out at the ocean before him and thought about the letter he had left for Pa: *I must follow my own dream. I hope to make you proud of me some day.*

Theatergoing in the 1800s

As Ira Aldridge was pursuing an acting career, theater was becoming a popular form of entertainment. For those New Yorkers who could afford a Saturday night on the town, the theater became their preferred destination. Theater was a place where white and black, wealthy and **working-class**, enslaved and free people came together. But they often had very different experiences—even though they were in the same building.

The wealthiest white New Yorkers pulled up in their horse-drawn carriages to the Park Theatre, the Bowery Theatre, or the Chatham Garden Theatre. They arrived well-dressed, **strutted** inside, and paid two dollars to sit in the expensive seats. Working-class white people went to the same theaters. For fifty cents, they sat in the back rows, under the balcony. They were not as well-mannered as the people in the expensive seats. They were rowdy and expressed their approval or disapproval of the performances loudly. Some of them chewed tobacco during performances and spat on the floor. Watching from the balcony were African Americans who had paid twenty-five cents for their

Interior of the Park Theatre, Manhattan, New York City.

seats. In the balcony, everyone sat together—rowdy beside well-mannered, **entrepreneurs** beside cooks and maids.

No matter where they sat, the theatergoers shared the danger of being caught in a crowded fire trap! The theaters, though beautiful and grand, were built with wood and lit with candles. This **combustible** combination made fires a common occurrence. The Park burned down in 1820 and was rebuilt in 1821. The African Grove had already closed when the building that housed it went up in flames in 1826. The Park burned down again in 1848 and was not rebuilt.

The ever-present threat of fire was not the only **hazard** patrons experienced. Many theaters, even the grand Park Theatre, were infested with rodents. A bell rang when it was time for the curtains to rise and the patrons to take their seats. Unfortunately, this bell also signaled dinnertime for the rats! As audience members sat munching on snacks, distracted by the events unfolding on stage, the crafty rodents went into action. They crept along the floor, sniffing out dropped peanuts and orange peels. Right on cue, when the final curtain fell, the rats disappeared.

Despite these risks, patrons eagerly settled down for the long night of entertainment ahead. Back then, audiences could expect to see a play, comedy act, and ballet in one sitting. An evening at the theater could last five or six hours! The audience members would be excited to hear their favorite songs and see familiar routines. The main act might be a Shakespearean play performed by the most famous actors of the day. Actors at that time had passionate fans just like popular stars today have dedicated followers. Sometimes the audience became as lively as a modern-day concert audience.

The enthusiasm that African American patrons had for theatre was different from other patrons. In the early nineteenth century, a night at the theater for black New Yorkers was a break from—and a reminder of—their new and **precarious** position in society. Almost every one of them, whether seated in the balcony of the Park or the front row of the Grove, was no more than one generation removed from slavery. For them, being at the theater, dressed in their finest, was recognition of how far they had come and a sign of hope for the future.

CHAPTER FOUR

FOLLOWING IN SHAKESPEARE'S FOOTSTEPS

Ira arrived in England two months later. He could not contain his joy as he skipped along London's cobblestone streets. "I am following in Shakespeare's footsteps!"

With help from the Wallack brothers, Ira found work running errands at a few small theaters. He was also hired to be an understudy. As an understudy, he had to be ready to take the part of any actor who, for some reason, could not perform.

Finally, after waiting many months, Ira got his chance. He was asked to replace an actor who had become ill. This marked the beginning of Ira's acting career in England.

Many theatergoers praised Ira's acting. Others were not so kind.

"He needs more training!" said some critics.

"He should not play roles intended for white actors," insisted others.

Ira could see that even in England his path to success would not be easy. But he was not discouraged. He worked hard, studied acting, and learned everything he could about the theater business. With each performance, Ira's acting improved. He became known for his ability to play a variety of roles.

For *The Merchant of Venice*, Ira put on a wig and makeup to **portray** Shylock, a character disliked because he was Jewish. As Shylock, Ira remembered the plight of his

own people back home when he asked:

If you prick us, do we not bleed?

If you tickle us, do we not laugh?

Even as Ira's dream was coming true, he never forgot about his people and the nightmare of slavery. Sometimes, at the close of a performance, Ira stepped out of character and sat on the edge of the stage.

He preached to the audience about the injustice of slavery. He told them that, although he was born free, he had once come close to being sold into slavery. Audiences were moved as Ira **recounted** for them the cruelties he had witnessed.

"I will not be satisfied," Ira said, "until all of my people are free."

He asked audience members to join him in sending money to help the abolitionists in the United States, who were fighting to free all those who were enslaved.

William Shakespeare

Born in 1564 in Stratford-upon-Avon, England, William Shakespeare was the oldest of John and Mary Shakespeare's six children. He had a typical childhood for a boy growing up in **Elizabethan** England. Young Will's education began when he was four years old. He set off each school day with his **hornbook** and a goose-feather **quill**.

Growing up, Will and the other students spent up to eight hours a day in class and they memorized long passages of poetry in Latin and Greek. They studied the works of ancient Roman scholars and writers. Will would later draw on the history and myths he learned in school to write the plays that would make him famous.

Although school was serious business, there were days when the students received a special treat. Once a year, a traveling group of actors, or *players*, arrived in Stratford-upon-Avon. Students were allowed to skip school and attend the outdoor performances. As young Will sat spellbound while watching a play unfold on a **makeshift** stage, he dreamed of becoming a playwright.

An engraving of William Shakespeare (1564-1616), published in Dugdale's *England and Wales Delineated*, United Kingdom, 1848.

When William was sixteen, he graduated from Stratford Grammar School. Since his parents could not afford to send him to college, he may have worked as a glovemaker in the family business, or as an assistant to a lawyer or schoolmaster.

In 1582, when he was eighteen years old, William married Anne Hathaway, a woman from a nearby village. They had three children. Their daughter Susanna was born in 1583, and their twins, Judith and Hamnet, arrived in 1585.

Even though William now had responsibilities as a husband and father, he still longed to work in the theater. But to do so, he would have to move to London, which was a noisy, dangerous, dirty, and overcrowded city at the time. It was no place to raise a family. Around 1590, William and Anne made the difficult decision for William to go to London while Anne and the children remained in Stratford. William would visit his family and send money home as often as possible.

The next time players arrived in Stratford, William volunteered to work for them by tending their horses, building sets, and making costumes. Impressed by William's hard work, the players asked him to join them. When it was time for the troupe to move on, William said goodbye to his family and began the 100-mile journey to London, where he quickly made a name for himself. He was active in all **aspects** of the theater: acting, building sets, and most importantly, writing.

William Shakespeare was a **prolific** writer. He wrote 154 sonnets—poems with 14 lines and 10 syllables per line—and 37 plays including romances, histories, comedies, and tragedies. As he spun tales of mistaken identities, love, revenge, magic, greed, jealousy, and murder, Shakespeare's own life was not without **misfortune**. In 1596, Shakespeare's son died. Hamnet was only 11 years old, but his death would not have been considered unusual. In Elizabethan England, an estimated 30 percent of children died before they reached the age of 15, often due to one of the deadly illnesses that were common at the time. Five years after William lost his son, his father died. William crafted some of his saddest plays after losing his father. Two examples are the tragedies *Hamlet* (1601) and *Othello* (1604).

William used a wide variety of characters, including royalty, ghosts, clowns, witches, spirits, and fairies in his plays. He had a gift for giving these characters just the right word or phrase to say. When such a term did not exist, he invented one "out of thin air"—a phrase he created. Shakespeare had several ways of creating new words. He joined two words together (*outbreak*), changed a noun into a verb (*elbow*), or added a prefix (*discontent)* or suffix (*eventful)*. Shakespeare invented dozens of words and phrases just for the four plays quoted in this book.

Here are a few of Shakespeare's inventions:

Hamlet	*Othello*
barefaced	addiction
besmirch	hint
friend (verb)	foregone conclusion
my heart of hearts	green-eyed monster (jealousy)
pander	wear my heart upon my sleeve

Romeo and Juliet	*The Merchant of Venice*
bump	Jessica (Shylock's daughter)
ladybird	compromise
star-crossed	laughable
uncomfortable	all that glitters is not gold
wild-goose chase	bated breath

All told, Shakespeare introduced over 1,700 words and phrases to the English language. Many of us quote Shakespeare without even knowing it!

Four hundred years after they were written, Shakespeare's plays, with their **universal** appeal, enduring themes, and beautiful words, are still read and performed all over the world. They have been translated into almost every language. Shakespeare left a remarkable **legacy** behind. After he died on April 23, 1616, he was **eulogized** by his friend and fellow writer, Ben Jonson, who wrote that William Shakespeare "was not of an age, but for all time!"

Shakespeare's Globe in London, Great Britain, today. This structure was partly inspired by the Globe Theatre, where many of Shakespeare's plays were performed throughout his lifetime. The original theater burned down during a performance of Shakespeare's *Henry VIII* in 1613. The modern Shakespeare's Globe opened in 1997.

CHAPTER FIVE
CELEBRATED ACTOR

Ira's fame and fortune grew as he traveled beyond England. Wherever he went, he worked with local actors and showed them how to make costumes and sets.

By the 1840s, Ira was one of the most celebrated Shakespearean actors in Europe. His most famous role was the lead character in *Othello*. The dark-skinned **tragic** hero was commonly played by a white actor wearing black makeup.

Ira did not need makeup. And the emotions he expressed as Othello were as real as the color of his skin. Like Othello, Ira knew despair. He had seen it in the eyes of enslaved people. And like Othello, Ira knew sadness and regret. He had felt both when he received news of Pa's death.

After many years of portraying Othello, Ira became the character in the minds of his admirers. They sat spellbound at his performances.

Ira seemed to speak directly to each person in the audience in the tragedy's final scene:

> When you shall these unlucky deeds relate,
>
> Speak of me as I am; nothing **extenuate,**
>
> ... Then must you speak
> Of one that loved not wisely but too well.

One night at London's famous Theatre Royal Haymarket, Ira received a standing **ovation** after another stirring performance of *Othello*. As he bowed before the **adoring** crowd, Ira realized that by following his dream, he had also become what Pa and Mr. Andrews had wanted him to be. He was an actor, but he was also a teacher and a preacher.

Ira smiled and took a final bow as the curtain closed.

Othello, the Moor of Venice

Inspired by the Italian play *Un Capitano Moro*, Shakespeare wrote the tragedy *Othello* in 1603. In the play, Othello is a respected and successful general in the Venetian army. But he is also a **Moor**, which is a term used during Shakespeare's time to describe a dark-skinned person. In seventeenth-century Venice, Italy, many people looked down on Moors. Nevertheless, Othello falls in love with Desdemona, the daughter of a rich and powerful Venetian senator. Desdemona's father, Brabantio, is furious when he finds out that his daughter has married a Moor. Only after Desdemona and Othello convince Brabantio of their genuine love for each other does the senator give the couple his blessing.

Othello has a spiteful and envious enemy named Iago, but Othello believes he is his friend. Through tricks and lies, Iago convinces the quick-tempered Othello that Desdemona has fallen in love with someone else. Othello becomes jealous and angry.

In a fit of rage, Othello kills his wife. Afterward, Othello discovers too late that Iago has deceived him and that Desdemona had been faithful to him. Othello is overcome with **remorse**. He sees no option but to kill himself. But before he commits this final, desperate act, he has one request. Othello asks that those who tell the story of his life neither **exaggerate** the events nor leave

Ira Aldridge as Othello

anything out. They should say that, although he had been foolish, he had cared for Desdemona dearly:

> **When you shall these unlucky deeds relate,**
> **Speak of me as I am; nothing extenuate,**
> **...Then must you speak**
> **Of one that loved not wisely but too well.**
> *Othello*, Act V, Scene 2:340-345

CHAPTER SIX
TRAILBLAZER

Although Ira never received the **recognition** in the United States that he earned abroad, he is considered one of the greatest Shakespearean actors of the nineteenth century. Among the roles he played were Macbeth, King Lear, Richard III, and, of course, Othello the Moor. Ira was the first black actor to portray Othello on the English stage.

Ira also found great fame in Germany, Russia, France, and other places outside of England. When performing in non-English-speaking countries, Ira spoke his lines in English while the local actors spoke their lines in their native language. Audiences loved this arrangement and were happy to hear Shakespeare's words in the language in which the plays had been written.

Ira was a vocal and generous supporter of the abolitionist movement in the United States. After the Civil War, and the abolition of slavery, he planned to make a **triumphant** return to his birthplace to perform at New York's Academy of Music. He also intended to take his wife and children to visit his native land and meet his family. But Ira did not live to see his plans realized. He died in 1867 at the age of sixty, in Lodz, Poland. His gravesite is still maintained by the Society of Polish Artists of Film and Theatre.

Ira received numerous awards during his lifetime, including the Gold Medal for Arts and Sciences from the king of Prussia. In 1858, the duke of Saxe-Meiningen (now in Germany) granted him knighthood.

Memorials to Aldridge can be found throughout the world. At Howard University in Washington, DC, a theater is named after him. But perhaps the greatest honor is a bronze plaque inscribed with his name at the Shakespeare Memorial Theatre, at Stratford-upon-Avon, England, the birthplace of William Shakespeare. Ira Aldridge is the only African American among the thirty-three actors to have received this recognition.

Ira Aldridge, circa 1865

TIMELINE

1807 July 24: Ira Frederick Aldridge is born in New York City, NY

1820 Enrolls at the African Free School

1824 Leaves the United States to pursue acting in England

1825 Marries an Englishwoman named Margaret Gill

1825 Makes his European stage debut in London

1840s Grows in popularity throughout Europe

1858 Granted knighthood by the duke of Saxe-Meiningen

1864 His wife, Margaret, dies of illness

1865 Marries an opera singer named Amanda von Brandt

1867 Dies in Lodz, Poland at age 59

1956 Theater named in his honor at Howard University

GLOSSARY

abolition (ab-oh-LIH-shun) *noun* the act of ending something permanently

adoring (a-DOOR-ing) *adjective* admiring

agony (a-guh-nee) *noun* extreme pain of the mind or body

alumni (a-LUM-ny) *noun* people who attended a specific school or university

American Revolution (a-MER-eh-ken rev-oh-LOO-shun) *proper noun* a rebellion lasting from 1775 to 1783 in which the American colonies won independence from Great Britain

aspects (ASS-peks) *noun* the parts of something

audition (aw-DIH-shun) *noun* a short presentation a performer gives to show off their talents and be considered for a role or part in a production

barreled (BARE-ruld) *verb* to move with great speed or force

benefactor (BEN-eh-fak-tor) *noun* a person who supports a person, organization, or cause, often by donating money

combustible (kom-BUS-tuh-bull) *adjective* able to burn easily

contemplating (KON-tem-play-ting) *verb* thinking

curriculum (ku-RIK-yew-lum) *noun* the classes taught by a school

dignitaries (DIG-neh-tare-eez) *plural noun* important people

distinction (dis-TINK-shun) *noun* quality or excellence

Elizabethan (ee-liz-ah-BEE-than) *adjective* taking place during the reign of Queen Elizabeth I of England (1558-1603)

engraver (in-GRAY-ver) *noun* a person who cuts or carves designs into a hard surface

entrepreneur (ahn-treh-pren-NOOR) *noun* a person who starts a business

eulogized (YU-lo-jized) *verb* to write or say kind and thoughtful things, usually about someone who has died

exaggerate (eks-AHJ-er-ate) *verb* to describe something as bigger or more significant than it actually is

extenuate (eks-TEN-yew-ate) *verb* to weaken or excuse something

founded (FOWN-ded) *verb* to create or establish something

harassed (ha-RASSED) *verb* to bother someone repeatedly

hazard (HAZ-erd) *noun* danger

hornbook (HORN-book) *noun* a tablet with the alphabet and numbers one through ten printed across the top, used to teach children writing

instilling (en-STILL-ing) *verb* to put a specific feeling or idea in someone's mind

legacy (LEG-ah-see) *noun* something received from someone in the past

liberated (lib-er-AY-ted) *adjective* set free

makeshift (MAYK-shift) *adjective* something that temporarily fills in for a thing of better quality

manumission (MAN-yew-mih-shun) *noun* the act of freeing enslaved people

melodic (mel-OH-dik) *adjective* musical

minister (MIN-ess-tur) *noun* the religious leader of a church

misfortune (miz-FOR-chun) *noun* bad luck

merchant (MUR-chant) *noun* a person who buys and sells things in large quantities

momentous (mo-MEN-tuss) *adjective* incredibly important

Moor (MOR) *noun* a term used during William Shakespeare's time to refer to a dark-skinned person

ovation (oh-VAY-shun) *noun* enthusiastic clapping and cheering

passersby (PASS-erz-by) *noun* people who walk past something on a street

playwright (PLAY-rite) *noun* a person who writes plays for the theater

portray (POOR-tray) *verb* to play or show

precarious (pree-KAR-ee-us) *adjective* unstable

prejudice (PREJ-oo-dis) *noun* a negative opinion formed for no reason; a dislike of people who are of a different religion, country, gender, or race

premier (pree-MEER) *adjective* the best or highest

prolific (pro-LIFF-ik) *adjective* productive

quill (KWIL) *noun* a writing tool made from a bird's feather

recognition (REK-og-nih-shun) *noun* credit or acknowledgement

recounted (ree-KOWN-ted) *verb* to describe a past event in detail

recital (REE-sy-tal) *noun* performance

remorse (REE-morss) *noun* a feeling of regret or guilt

reviled (re-VY-uld) *verb* hated

rigorous (RIG-or-us) *adjective* very difficult or challenging

ruckus (RUK-us) *noun* a noisy commotion

scolding (SKOL-ding) *verb* to speak in an angry way to someone who did something wrong

segregate (seg-ree-GATE) *verb* to separate people of different groups, particularly based on race

spellbound (SPEL-bownd) *adjective* charmed or captivated

stagestruck (STAYJ-struk) *adjective* fascinated by theater

steward (STOO-erd) *noun* a person who is responsible for the comfort of passengers traveling on a ship or airplane

strutted (STRUT-ted) *verb* to walk in a confident way that attracts attention

summarize (SUM-er-ize) *verb* to explain something in a few words

tragic (TRAJ-ik) *adjective* extremely sad or disastrous, as in a *tragedy*—a play focusing on sad events

triumphant (try-UM-fant) *adjective* victorious

tryst (TRIST) *noun* a secret meeting between lovers

universal (u-neh-VER-sall) *adjective* applying to all people or situations

valet (VAH-lay) *noun* a male personal servant

venue (VEN-yoo) *noun* a place where a performance or event happens

whitewashing (WHITE-wah-shing) *verb* the act of making a surface whiter by using a white liquid

working-class (WERK-ing klass) *adjective* making money doing physical work

TEXT SOURCES

Hampson, Norma. "A Visit From Ira Aldridge." Shakespeare.org. https://www.shakespeare.org.uk/ explore-shakespeare/blogs/visit-ira-aldridge/

Hill, Errol G., and James Vernon Hatch. *A History of African American Theatre*. Cambridge University Press, 2003.

Howard.edu. "Welcome to Howard University!" Accessed December 4, 2018. https://www.howard. edu/explore/self-guided-tour.pdf

"Ira Aldridge 1807–1867." Biography Resource Center. http://www.lib.subr.edu/BLACK_HISTORY/ Aldridge, _Ira_Frederick_3.pdf

Lindfors, Bernth. *Ira Aldridge: The African Roscius*. Rochester, NY: University of Rochester Press, 2007.

Malone, Mary. *Actor in Exile: The Life of Ira Aldridge*. London, UK: Crowell-Collier Press, 1969.

Marshall, Herbert, and Mildred Stock. *Ira Aldridge: The Negro Tragedian*. Washington, DC: Howard University Press, 1993.

Shakespeare, William. *The Complete Works of William Shakespeare*. New York: Barnes & Noble Books, 1994. Citations refer to the Barnes & Noble edition.

Williams, Michael. "Aldridge, Ira (1807–1867)." BlackPast. org: Remembered & Reclaimed. http://www. blackpast.org/aah/aldridge-ira-1807-1867#sthash. A2BRV7lF.dpuf

SIDEBAR SOURCES

THE AFRICAN FREE SCHOOL

Andrews, Charles C. *History of the New-York African Free-Schools*. 1830. Reprint, London: Forgotten Books, 2015.

Berlin, Ira, and Leslie M. Harris, eds. *Slavery in New York*. New York: The New Press, 2005.

Bernard, Sheila Curran, and Sarah Mondale. *School: The Story of American Public Education*. Boston: Beacon Press, 2001.

New York Historical Society. "Examination Days: The New York African Free School Collection: Introduction: The New York African Free School." Accessed January 30, 2019. https://www.nyhistory.org/web/africanfreeschool/history/

———. "Examination Days: The New York African Free School Collection: The New York Manumission Society." Accessed January 30, 2019. https://www.nyhistory.org/web/africanfreeschool/history/manumission-society.html

———. "P.S. 1: Old School (Literally)." Published January 17, 2012. https://nyhistorywalks.wordpress.com/2012/01/17/p-s-1-old-school-literally/

Peterson, Carla L. *Black Gotham: A Family History of African Americans in Nineteenth Century New York City*. New Haven and London: Yale University Press, 2011.

Smith, James McCune. Introduction to *A Memorial Discourse by Reverend Henry Highland Garnet*. Philadelphia: J. M. Wilson, 1865.

Thomas, J. D. "New York's African Free Schools in Freedom's Journal in 1828." Accessible Archives. Posted on April 2, 2012. https://www.accessible-archives.com/2012/04/new-yorks-african-free-schools-in-freedoms-journal-in-1828/

White, Shane. *Stories of Freedom in Black New York*. Cambridge and London: Harvard University Press, 2002.

THE AFRICAN GROVE THEATRE

Alexander, Leslie M. *African or American? Black Identity and Political Activism in New York City, 1784-1861*. Chicago: University of Illinois Press, 2008.

Berlin, Ira, and Leslie M. Harris, eds. *Slavery in New York*. New York: The New Press, 2005.

McAllister, Marvin. *White People Do Not Know How to Behave at Entertainments Designed for Ladies & Gentlemen of Colour: William Brown's African and American Theater*. Chapel Hill and London: The University of North Carolina Press, 2003.

Peterson, Carla L. *Black Gotham: A Family History of African Americans in Nineteenth Century New York City*. New Haven and London: Yale University Press, 2011.

Taylor, Erica. "African Grove Theatre." *Black Americaweb.com*. Accessed on January 30, 2019. https://blackamericaweb.com/2011/08/03/african-grove-theatre/

White, Shane. *Stories of Freedom in Black New York*. Cambridge and London: Harvard University Press, 2002.

THEATERGOING IN THE 1800S

Barger, Andrew, ed. *Entire Tales and Poems of Edgar Allan Poe: Photographic and Annotated Edition*. Collierville, TN: Bottletree Books, 2006.

McAllister, Marvin. *White People Do Not Know How to Behave at Entertainments Designed for Ladies & Gentlemen of Colour: William Brown's African and American Theater*. Chapel Hill and London: The University of North Carolina Press, 2003.

Peterson, Carla L. *Black Gotham: A Family History of African Americans in Nineteenth Century New York City*. New Haven and London: Yale University Press, 2011.

WILLIAM SHAKESPEARE

Chrisp, Peter. *Eyewitness SHAKESPEARE*. London: DK Publishing, 2004.

Lepscky, Ibi. *William Shakespeare*. New York: Barron's Educational Series, 1988.

Mabillard, Amanda. "Shakespeare online." Accessed January 2, 2019. http://www.shakespeare-online.com/

Marche, Stephen. *How Shakespeare Changed Everything*. New York: Harper Perennial, 2011.

Middleton, Haydn. *What's Their Story: William Shakespeare*. New York: Oxford University Press, 1977.

Shakespeare's Globe. "Original Globe." Accessed March 27, 2019. https://www.shakespearesglobe.com/ about-us/history-of-the-globe/rebuilding-the-globe

———. "Rebuilding the Globe." Accessed March 27, 2019. https://www.shakespearesglobe.com/about-us/ history-of-the-globe/original-globe

Stanley, Diane and Peter Vennema. *Bard of Avon: The Story of William Shakespeare*. New York: Morrow Junior Books, 1992.

OTHELLO, THE MOOR OF VENICE

Shakespeare, William. *The Complete Works of William Shakespeare*. New York: Barnes & Noble Books, 1994.

RECOMMENDED FURTHER READING

Fiction books are marked with an asterisk.

SHAKESPEARE

* Blackwood, Gary. *The Shakespeare Stealer*. Reprint. New York: Puffin Books, 2000.

* Carbone, Courtney, and William Shakespeare. *Srsly Hamlet*. New York: Random House, 2015.

* Chevalier, Tracy. *New Boy: William Shakespeare's Othello Retold*. New York: Hogarth, 2017.

* Cooper, Susan. *King of Shadows*. New York: McElderry Books, 1999.

* Hinds, Gareth. *Romeo & Juliet*. Somerville, MA: Candlewick, 2013.

Mannis, Celeste. *Who Was William Shakespeare?* Who Was. New York: Grosset & Dunlap, 2006.

THEATER AND PERFORMANCE

Belli, Mary Lou, and Dinah Lenney. *Acting For Young Actors: The Untlimate Teen Guide*. New York: Backstage Books, 2006.

* Federle, Tim. *Better Nate Than Never*. New York: Simon & Schuster, 2013.

Greenfield, Eloise. *Paul Robeson*. New York: Lee & Low Books, 2009.

* Keenan-Bolger, Andrew, and Kate Wetherhead. *Jack & Louisa Act 1*. New York: Penguin Random House, 2015.

* Mientus, Andy. *The Backstagers and the Ghost Light*. Illustrated by Rian Sygh. New York: Harry N. Abrams, 2018.

* Streitfeld, Noel. *Theater Shoes*. Reprint. New York: Yearling, 1994.

* Telgemeier, Raina. *Drama*. New York: Scholastic, 2012.

ABOUT THE AUTHOR AND ILLUSTRATOR

GLENDA ARMAND won Lee & Low's New Voices Award in 2006 for her book *Love Twelve Miles Long* and has worked for many years as a teacher and school librarian in Los Angeles, California. Glenda loves reading about history and is passionate about sharing the stories of African Americans and little-known historical figures. She now lives in Los Angeles, California. Glenda can be found on the web at glenda-armand.com.

FLOYD COOPER is an award-winning illustrator who has been recognized with three Coretta Scott King Illustrator Honors and the Illustrator Award for *The Blacker the Berry*. Born and raised in Tulsa, Oklahoma, he came to New York in 1984 to pursue a career in illustration. Cooper is known for his unique artistic technique that involves erasing oil washes from boards to create images. He now lives in Easton, Pennsylvania, with his family.